The Human Face

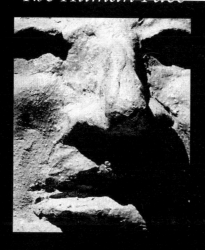

FREDERICK FRANCK

Ode To
The Human Face

Foreword

MARVIN BARRETT

Photography

LUZ PIEDAD LOPEZ

Design

MARTIN MOSKOF

CODHILL PRESS • NEW PALTZ • NEW YORK

Text, Copyright © 2004 by Frederick Franck
Photographs, Copyright © 2004 by Luz P. Lopez
Design, Copyright © 2004 Martin Moskof

All rights reserved. No part of this book may be reproduced or transmitted in any form or
by any means, electronic or mechanical, including photocopying, recording, or by any infor-
mation storage and retrieval system, without permission in writing from the Publisher.

•

Library of Congress Cataloging-in Publication Data

Franck, Frederick, 1909-
    Ode to the human face: masks and aphorisms on that which matters/
    Frederick Franck; designed by Martin Moskof ; photographs by Luz Piedad Lopez.
    p. cm.
  ISBN 1-930337-12-4 (alk. paper)
1. Spiritual life. I. Title
BL624.F7195 2004
128--dc22

                        2003055735

Limited Edition of 900 copies
Printed by BookMobile in the U.S.A. • July 2004

A Dedication

*What could be more relevant, more important than to answer the question
what does it mean to be human?
I dedicate this book to Paul D. MacLean MD * whom I regard as one of the most
brilliant and definitely most humanly relevant scientists of our time. It is the noble
achievement of MacLean to have rehabilitated the meaning of the epithet "human"
in terms of modern neuro-science. Dr. MacLean coined the term The Triune Brain
to characterize the structure of the human brain. In his thirty-five years of research
he came to regard the prefrontal cortex, the most recent outcropping of the brain's cortex,
to be its humanizing function, for it enables us to be aware as the only species, of its
limited life span, of its mortality, as well as sensitizing us to the mortality, the pain,
the suffering of other living creatures. Thus the first inklings of empathy can arise and
from empathy to compassion is but a step.
One might conclude that the capacity for compassion is that which differentiates the
pre-human, the anthropoid in us, from Anthropos, the Truly Human.
Could it be that the figures of the Buddha and the Christ are the living paradigms
of Wisdom/Compassion?
I honor Paul MacLean as being the contemporary scientist who, by purely scientific terms**
reconfirmed the metaphysical insights into Reality, what Karl Jaspers named the Axial
Period between 500 BC and 200 AD, when the great religious traditions took form.*

—Frederick Franck

*Chief, Laboratory of Brain Evolution and Behavior, National Institute of Mental Health
**"To Be Human Against All Odds" Frederick Franck 1991

Foreword

It is more than appropriate that Frederick Franck should call this remarkable sequence of clay sculptures and the revelatory commentary that accompanies them "Ode to the Human Face" - a poetic application. If Wilfrid Owen's affirmation that "the poetry is in the pity" is true, and I believe it is, Franck's visual poetry is underscored and justified by a pity that has characterized an astounding variety of activities throughout his long life. Examining the pages that follow one senses that there is more to these rough-hewn visages than their apparently cruel power that strikes one at first glance.

"Heaven arms with pity those whom it would not see destroyed" Lao Tse's admonition uttered millennia before Owen's might be a more appropriate justification for these images and indeed for all the activities which have occupied the artist-author into his tenth decade.

Looking at the life and accomplishments which have led up to the current volume one would be inclined to call Franck "a Renaissance man" if the term were not both inadequate and sorely over-applied. Today anyone with a fair competence in two or three disciplines is automatically awarded the title. Franck with a dozen cultivated talents and skills would better be termed "a universal man" or "a man for all seasons" with a double emphasis on the "all."

Over the years Franck's concerns, medical, artistic, literary, metaphysical, social, have made his life an incomparably full and challenging one both for himself and the viewers, readers, patients and spiritual seekers who have been touched by them.

As in so many cases Franck's multiple vocations and the overarching pity that informed them had their origins in his childhood.

To the war that inspired Owen's poetry and claimed his life, Franck was a youthful witness.

From his upstairs window in the family home in Maastricht, the Netherlands, the five year old witnessed the devastating procession of the Great War's victims passing in the street below, wounded men, women, old men and children clutching a few prized possessions, fleeing the ravages of a brutal, senseless conflict. Seeing this pathetic parade the child sensed there was no alternative but peace, and compassion. He never deviated from those convictions.

The titles of a handful of his thirty five published works give some indication of the multi-laned road Franck chose to take. "My Eye Is In Love", "Pilgrimage to Now/Here", "Fingers Pointing Toward the Sacred", "To Be Human Against All Odds."

"Days with Albert Schweitzer" chronicles the three years he spent assisting the great man at his African clinic. "Outsider in the Vatican" gives witness to Franck's extended presence during the heady days of Vatican II and   his lifelong admiration for   Pope John XXIII. "The Zen of Seeing" and a half dozen other titles are the fruit of visits to Japan and a demonstration of his openness to religious traditions other than the Catholicism of his native milieu. "Pacem in Terris. A Love Story" is his tribute to his bucolic headquarters in Warwick, New York, established forty years ago and still a flourishing center devoted to art, music and peace.

Franck's formidable pilgrimage is recorded not only in books but in a sequence of works of art: pen and ink drawings of an exquisite specificity, paintings that display a technical mastery and a breadth of subject matter from the abstract to the hauntingly real, from poignant studies of the nude to a recent series that lifts the veil on a wise man's glimpse of eternity.

Still as "An Ode to the Human Face" bears witness, Franck has never turned his back on his fellow man. Observations begun in the parlors and squares of his childhood home, are still recognizable all these years later.

Not that there is anything stereotypical about these bits of clay or their stunning insights. Made with the manipulation of thumb and forefinger they convey eloquently in the simplest vocabulary what people think and feel and betray with eyes, mouth, cheeks, temples and chin. There they all are behind their transparent masks, the haughty and the humble, the puzzled and the knowing, the mindlessly cheerful and the deeply distressed, the smug, the skeptical, the pretentious, the devout and the judgmental, the dolt and the sage, the martyr and the visionary.

"In every face there are traces visible of those components of the ego that cause the blackout of the "Light that lightens everyone come into the world, which distorts and disfigures the Original Face, the True Self" Franck writes in one of his many illuminating captions.

There you have it. Lao Tse's, Owen's and now Franck's insight that always there underneath is the firm reconciler of all, the preserver of life, the pity.

Marvin Barrett
Author, Senior Editor *Parabola*

This book came about as unexpectedly as a snowstorm in August.

A few weeks ago my son Lukas, looking for a tool in the jumble under my workbench found a few cardboard boxes filled with small clay faces which I had molded over the years, often just a few inches in diameter. They touched him by their impact, their obvious spontaneity, and so we started to look at them together under my reading magnifier, an appliance without which I can not read anymore.

Our friend Luz Piedad, that passionate photographer, happened to be around and at once, fascinated, she started to focus on these faces. A few days later she had printed almost a hundred of her photographs, and even enlarged them.

They were a revelation, a pulsing sequence of contemplations on the human face, a fugue on the human theme.

Not a single one of the clay variations on that theme was done with an ulterior motive, any thought about an exhibition and even less a book in mind.

Still now, in my ninety-fifth year on earth, my eyesight impaired, already quite deaf, I could not resist imagining this fugue transcribed into a sequence of words and images. My swan-song of images hardly needs any words. They will speak clearly for themselves or they will not.

I kept playing with these photographs in a variety of sequences for days. They struck me as instant responses to faces that had affected, captivated, shocked, frightened me in a bus, a plane, a coffee-shop, at a traffic light perhaps.

They had kept haunting me, until – at some odd moment – my fingers seemed as it were compulsively to start modeling them in any material at hand, be it clay, wax or water putty, interrupting whatever else I was working on. The clay ones were fired in a friend's kiln.

I felt them to be directly related to my life-long intense preoccupation with the meaning of being born human, in other words: Who am I? Who are you? I even wrote a few books trying to solve that riddle.

Did my fugue of faces somehow answer the ultimate question in its own non-verbal way?

Most of these archetypal faces – "they might be Neolithic, Etruscan, pre-historic, thousands of years old," people said, "but undeniably human, at the very least potentially so."

Some are indeed a mere few inches in diameter. Others, however, became life-size and were integrated in one of those three-dimensional "sculptures" in steel, wood, stone, that at times I am driven to make. I do not really regard them as "sculptures", but rather as "icons," as "windows onto the Real, the Sacred," non-dogmatic reflections on That Which Matters. I am anything but a philosopher or theologian, less able to think in intellectual concepts than in symbolic imagery.

In contradiction to Descartes' "I think, therefore I am" I can only mumble "I SEE, therefore I am," being a compulsive image-maker by nature.

Looking through those many clay faces I tried to remember whose they were. I recognized at once that wretched old woman in her wheelchair, navigating a supermarket and the not so much younger, high-heeled lady in pastel mink, exploring Saks Fifth Avenue for the latest disguise of her sagging body; the double-chinned face of the bore sitting next to me, holding forth for hours in a 747; the angry stare of the white-haired professor, resenting being questioned after his lecture; the faces of women who bewitched me, when they and I were young, their once irresistible mating masks turned bitter-sweet. Each face is hiding the Ultimate Mystery of its Existence - as such - behind a quick succession of masks, each one intending to handle life's quiddities: the surgeon's frown of infallible competence, the Reverend's smirk of benevolence, the hostess's frozen smile.

My life-long preoccupation with the human mask and its revelations must have started very early indeed.

I was born on the Dutch-Belgian border in 1909, the fateful year that Louis Blériot was the first non-bird to fly across the Channel. It was the very spot where World War I exploded when I was five years old: a significant location and moment to start a life that would, by sheer miracle, outlast this bloodiest of centuries.

For on August 4, 1914, I was awakened by the opening salvos of the 20th century starting in earnest. The Kaiser's armies had invaded Belgium, half a mile from our doorstep. The German field guns booming all too nearby , set our house atremble. From my attic window, in horror, I watched the little city of Visé burning under a scarlet sky. Almost at once the endless files of wretched people fleeing their burning villages, wounded and dying soldiers on pushcarts and trucks, were crossing the border into Holland, which managed to remain neutral in this First World War. Looking down from our second floor window, I saw people carrying children and belongings on their backs. I still see – eighty eight years later as if it were this morning – the old man carrying his canary in a cage. He looked up at me. I stood there crying, a little bunch of grapes in my hand and threw a few of them to him, in a gesture of desperate compassion. And so from my fifth to my ninth year I was peering into hell from our neutral grandstand, sickened by that incurable, life-long allergy to war, to all physical violence.

It was in second grade that I spotted the little German bi-plane above our schoolyard, saw the pilot look down from his open cockpit, all leather cap and goggles who, violating our neutral airspace, dropped his bomb. It landed close to where I stood, but failed to explode.

Thanks to a sequence of such merciful malfunctions I outlived almost the full length of the century, surviving its continuum of mass murder, and even Franco, Hitler, Stalin, Mao, and their ghoulish ilk, who massacred millions in this beastly century that was – almost inconceivably – also that of Gandhi, Albert Schweitzer, Martin Luther King, Pope John XXIII, among many less known incarnations of humanness, who answered the central riddle of what it might mean to be human with their very lives, that central question to which all other ones, whether political, economic, religious, artistic, are peripheral.

We lived in the center of the ancient city of Maastricht, just a few steps from its charming town square bordered with linden trees. Here people strolled on balmy evenings and stood chatting after Sunday Mass in the gothic basilica

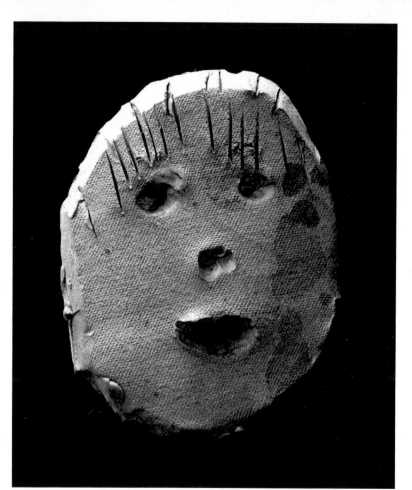

that dominated the square. It became my first observation post of the human face. Some ninety years later I still recall dozens of their masks in vivid detail. Echoes of some of these flashed back in this iconography.

I wonder whether these dozens of clay faces I molded could betray my premature critical fascination with all those physiognomies, so wondrous and so disquieting. Could it have been a primal fear, an existential *angst,* a defense against the grinning false faces of grown-ups, bending over one with their appropriate toothy grins, their sugary little frowns?

In my teens our town was still solidly – almost tribally - Catholic. One could not "join" the Church, "become" a Catholic. One might be warmly welcomed, but as a "convert," remain labeled a convert until the end, including in one's obituary.

People's masks were programmed to take on the proper pious expressions at any particular moment churchy stage directions prescribed them. The adhesive of the devout post-communion mask proved easily soluble in the correct quantities of gin or Heineken's, dispensed in the dozen cafés around the square, strictly, be it mutely, classified according to their "standing".

Café Dominicain, for instance, was archetypically bourgeois, and so were its clients' placid masks. The noisier café next door was borderline working class. Café Métropole was plebeian, sub-class. Café DuCasque, on the contrary, was unmistakably "better class." Here the elite sat stiffly in pin-striped distinction, exchanging fine-tuned smiles and bows, acknowledged with reserved benevolence or else with carefully graded subservient mimicry.

As to the art of bowing: it required bending one's lumbar spine to the appropriate degree, the neck remaining rigid, the mask expressionless as in a military salute, lips pressed together. Less formal bows called for the eyebrows to be raised almost imperceptibly, lips subtly relaxed into a semi-smile.

The technique of bowing to fit correctly any occasion required intense training before facing the kangaroo court of formidable high-bosomed ladies in ocelot coats to be approved of or flunked as a "well-brought-up young man" with a

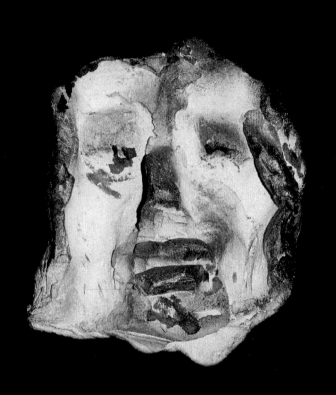

nod of their complex headgear. They are all forgotten, turned to dust and dande-lions long ago. Still, some seem to survive among my clay faces of this swan-song.

I left my hometown for the University when I was seventeen. By that time I had already gathered an impressive mental encyclopedia, so to speak, of human faces and their masks which had fascinated me practically from the time I was still rocking in my cradle, learning to smile on command as an introductory course in developing the subtle hypocrisy assumed to be indispensable for a successful life. When in 1938 I crossed the Atlantic and became a post-graduate student at Pittsburgh University, I dis-covered that my so very European encyclopedia of faces and masks was trans-atlanti-cally surprisingly valid and a useful guide indeed.

The first time I saw Richard Nixon on TV I had his number. He fitted my encyclopedia, was the spitting image of the self-satisfied importer of French wines to be served with liturgical solemnity in our most prestigious restaurants.

It was in Pittsburgh, after Pearl Harbor, that I became aware of the "manometer," the pressure gauge, imbedded somewhere in my organism. Its nee-dle had to be watched constantly. That very civilized looking couple, unmasked by their third Martini, might reveal itself as fanatical racist, "America First" fas-cistoid, that made the manometer needle jump all the way down – via pre-human, anthropoid, anti-human, to Red: "Mortal Danger!"

Drawing, modeling faces, I seem to touch my model's ancestral, even its pre-human, hominid past, that first hint of human Existence - of just being here - that Mystery of mysteries. Buddhism speaks in a minor key of Sun-yata , Absolute Nothingness, an Emptiness, however, replete with potentiali-ties, referred to in more positive terms as Tathata, Suchness.

Behind each personality, each mask, there is the irreducible Reality of Sunyata, of that all transcending Emptiness or Nothingness from which all that is, emerges in its Being/NonBeing.

This may well sound a bit complicated, even in my own ears. Trying to clarify it I failed and did not even notice that I had fallen into a daydream that took me to 7th Century China:

I saw myself knocking at Hui Neng's door. It opened slightly and I saw the patriarch standing there, tight-lipped. He confronted me with the question he often posed to aspirant Zen disciples, before accepting or rejecting them: "Show me your Original Face you had before even your parents were born."

I knew somehow by hearsay that this Original Face was the purely human dimension of the faces of which I had been kneading their everyday masks.

Hui Neng repeated his standard question: "Show me the Original Face…"

I could not speak.

He then thrust a mirror into my hands and said: "Go and keep watching! Be sure you remain aware of what you are looking for."

I sat down on a cot, staring into that mirror and what I saw horrified me, nauseated me to the point of vomiting.

But I kept watching, overcoming my nausea. I saw that ugly ape-like face with its bald head and ugly nose. I kept on watching. I saw it distorted in anger, in rage, I saw it grimacing in smiles and flatteries, in violent outbursts of aggression and hate until, very slowly, the image in my mirror began to go out of focus and after a few more hours becoming vague, featureless, its contour evaporated.

And I saw the No-Thingness that is the Original Face I must have had before even my parents were born.

In a wild joy I ran to Hui Neng's room and knocked.

He asked through the closed door : "Have you seen anything?"

All I could say was: "I have seen Nothing, Master!"

He opened the door and seemed to smile.

May I come back, may I stay?" I asked.

He did not answer, but kept smiling and just pointed at my mirror saying: "Go! Be aware of what you are looking for!" and closed the door.

—Hui Neng, 7th Century, Sixth Patriarch of Zen Buddhism.

Molding one of these faces I sometimes feel I am molding a karma, not limited to this particular face, but shared as if from the beginningless beginning

It is as if through this one face,
the entire past and present of our
species discloses itself; its
Original Face, as Zen calls it,
its specific Humanness,
mortal yet timeless.

This is obviously not a beauty contest.
It is a sequence of human faces as they struck me.
Indeed each one human, yet tainted to some degree,
by what in Christian tradition is known
as the seven capital sins:
pride, covetousness, lust, envy, gluttony, anger, sloth,
as formulated in the 6th C. by Pope Gregory the Great
and further clarified in the
13th century by Thomas Aquinas.
They may be seen as components of the
illusion-ridden predatory ego.

*"The spiritual life
is pain
raised
above the level
of
mere sensation."*

—*Daisetz T. Suzuki.*

When this spirituality
turns into conceptualization,

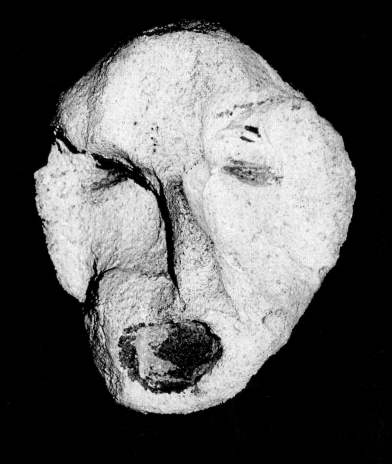

it congeals at once into the

antagonisms of the religions.

THE GREAT WISDOM

IS THE

GREAT COMPASSION

—*Mahakaruna*

THE GREAT COMPASSION

IS THE

GREAT WISDOM

—*Mahaprajna*

THE ESSENCE OF BUDDHISM

"God has imprinted on the human heart
a law his conscience bids him to obey."

JOHN XXIII, *"Pacem in Terris"*

*That law must be the Law of
human life in the Human mode,
the Dharma.*

We will not return to dirt, but to Earth, the Sacred, the desecrated, the violated. Where Earth is seen as dirt, the

bulldozer is destined to rule, to mutilate, to "develop",
to "landscape" what is considered as mere "dirt."

We may all be born genetically human — as indeed we are, regardless of how many of us are born — but this does not automatically confer the honorific "human" on us.

One cannot claim it by behaving like a rat or a copperhead and then excuse oneself with: "Ah, it's just human nature!" Acting like a snake or a rat is not human nature at all. It is snake nature or rat nature, no matter how much it is rationalized or whitewashed. Little wonder that when it becomes acceptable as normal conduct, society turns into a snake pit or a rat hole.

To be human against all odds — or not to be — is our crucial predicament.

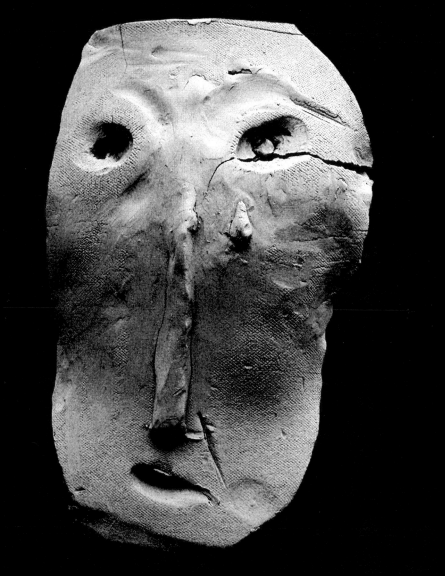

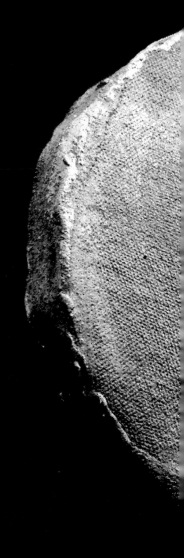

Yisan said to a monk
pining for enlightenment:
"I have nothing
to give you.
But if I would try,
you would be right
to laugh in my face,
for whatever
I could tell you
is my own;
it could never
be yours."

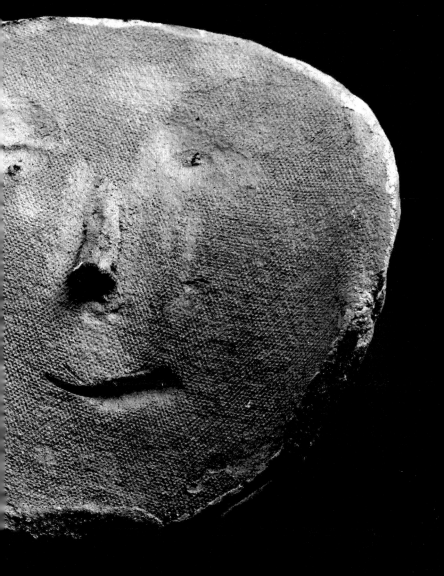

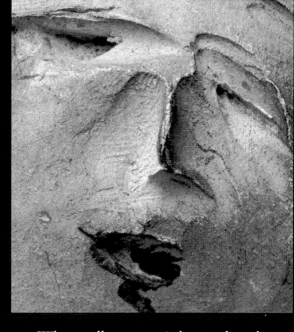

What really matters is how to live the human life, that means to distinguish strictly between the anthropoid, the hominid, the pre-human in us and what is fully human

Do not distrust your deepest intuitions.

You are not alone.

You are not mad!

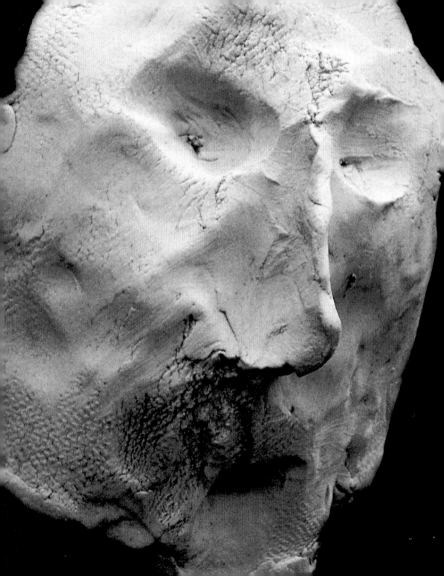

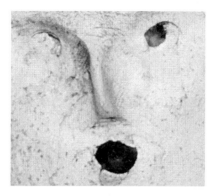

You are not losing your Way!
You are on your Way
You are your Way!

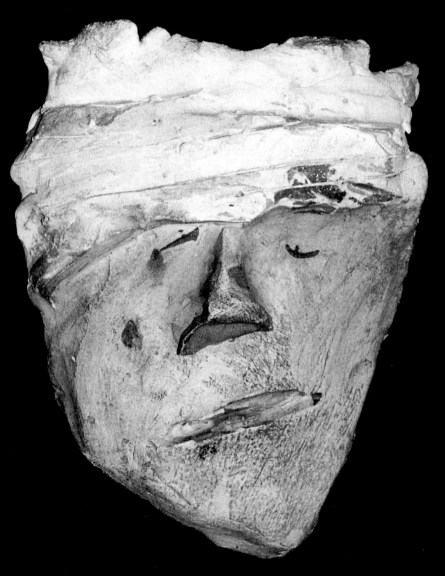

"If the
doors of perception were
cleansed,"
say William Blake,
"everything would
appear to man
as it is:
infinite."

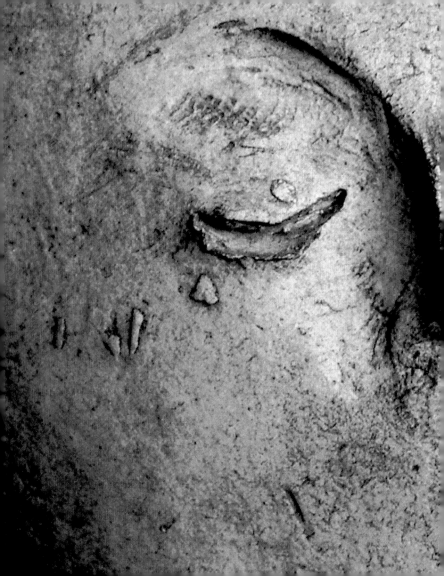

Real spirituality is the process
of the still pre-human
atavisms in us,
maturing into the fully Human:
Buddha Nature.
Spirit of Christ.

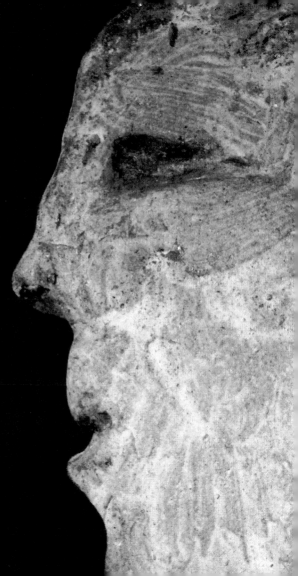

As I understand the Gospel, according to Thomas, it commands us to answer the question:
"Where do you really come from?"
with
"We come from the Light where It originated through Itself."

Life has hardly started...

*Once, while drawing an apple tree— thinking of
nothing, just watching, seeing, following that life
story through roots, trunk, branches, twigs—
the most baffling riddles solve themselves.
The tree became humankind rooted deep in the
earth, its limbs were the races, its twigs the families.
I, who once believed myself to be a tree, saw myself
as just one of the myriad
leaves of one long season— to be blown away
a little earlier, a little later.
Some other leaves had already fallen, many
remained stunted, some were still freshly
green in October.
But soon the November storms would
sweep us all away.*

The spiritual life is not an addition to
but the core of any life meriting
to be regarded as human.

*Identification
with a
fellow creature's
suffering
is called
compassion.*

Nicholas of Cusa:
"In all faces can be seen the Face of faces,
veiled as in a riddle."

The most recent outcropping in the
evolution of the human brain
is that prefrontal cortex,
which makes us the only animal
aware of our mortality,
of our short life span.

This enables us to feel
the first inklings of empathy
with other living beings.
From empathy to compassion
is but a step.
And voilá, we are human.
Could true compassion
be the central criterion
of being human?

When we return to where we have
always been
we do not have to ask what it means
when it is said of a man
he is so human
of a woman
she is a real human being.
So do not ask,
for we all know it,
just as we know
this water is cold, is warm;
this fruit is sweet, is sour
we know what it is to be human
and what is less.
It does not need explanation!

In every face the Face of faces is indeed discernable, but also in every face there are traces visible of those components of the ego that cause the blackout of the "Light that lightens everyone come into the world", of the True Self.

*Do not compute
eternity
as light-year
after year.
One step across
that line
called Time –
Eternity is here.*

—ANGELUS SILESIUS

You shall not worry about being of your own time,
for you are your time,
and it is brief!

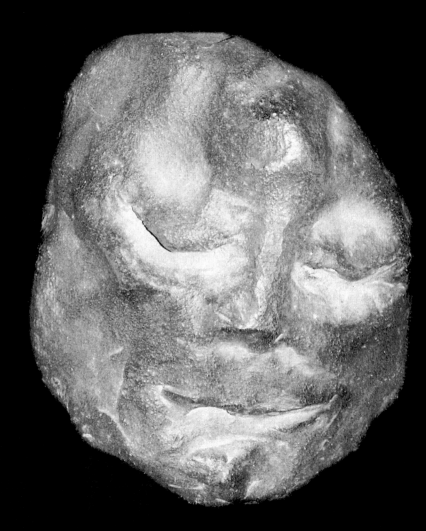

Forgive them
for
they see not
what they
look-at.
How could they
know
what they do.

I see the Face of faces,
see that the plural of man does not exist
is our cruelest hallucination
see our Oneness as infinite differentiation
see that the pattern of the universe and mine
are not-two
that what lives in me is the Tao in which all lives.
This is not what I believe
but the miracle my eyes saw on the Way.

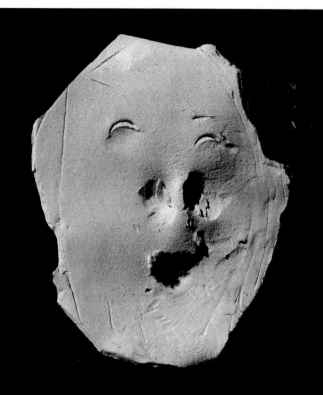

"Never fight evil as if it were something that
arose totally outside yourself."
—St. Augustine

*The anthropoid, outfitted with
modern technology is more destructive,
more murderous than any reptile,
any dragon ever imagined.*

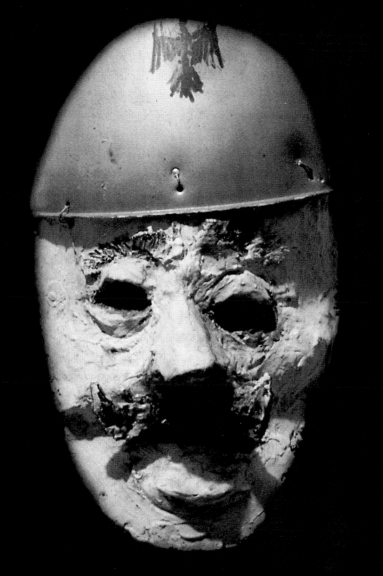

Albert Schweitzer had the insight in 1915 that "Reverence for Life" was the one principle on which all viable ethics could be grounded. He lived this principle every day as his life's motto until his death in 1965. Rachel Carson quoted him in her trail-blazing book "Silent Spring": "Man has lost the capacity to foresee and to forestall. He will end by destroying the earth."

*That what we
now ascribe to
the functioning of
the right brain,
is what from time
immemorial
has been spoken of
as coming from
the heart.*

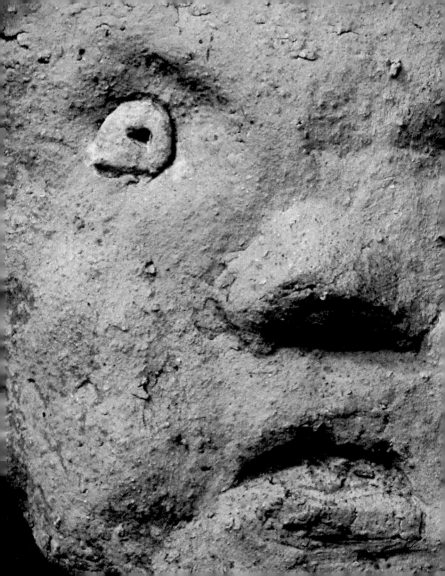

"*If we take eternity
to mean
not infinite
temporal duration,
but timelessness,
the eternal life
belongs to those
who live
in the present,*"
says
Wittgenstein

From pre-human
to the Human —
from anthropoid to Anthropos —
is but one step.
But it is this step
that marks each one's life.

Where it fails,
the ode becomes
bitter lament.

Where it succeeds,
the human is celebrated
in its fullness.

Acknowledgements in Gratitude

The meaning of life is to see. *Hui Neng*

If you use It, It will make you live. If you don't, It will destroy you.
The Gospel according to Thomas

As far as the Buddha Nature is concerned, there is no difference between sinner
and sage. . . .One enlightened insight and one is a Buddha, one foolish thought
and one is a common man again. *Hui Neng*

In every soul, even that of the greatest sinner, God dwells and is
substantially present. *Saint John of the Cross*

Become angry and you turn the Unborn, the Buddha Mind, into a Fighting
Demon, vent your selfishness and change it into a Hungry Ghost, give rise to
your folly and make it into an animal. *Bankei*

If you seek the Buddha outside of yourself, the Buddha turns into a devil.
Dogen

Your treasure house is within you. It contains all you need. *Hui Hai*

God is my Ground, I am God's Ground. *Meister Eckhart*

Nothingness Thou art/fathomless Abyss.
To see Abyss in all that is/is seeing that which is. *Angelus Silesius*

Blind my eyes and I can see Thee
Block my ears and I can hear Thee
And without feet I can go to Thee.
Rainer Maria Rilke